THE IMPACT OF BELIEF:
LEARNING TO TAKE CONTROL OF YOUR LIFE

Books by Lin Conklin

Choices in the Great Circle

The Power of Choice: Creating the Life You Want

THE IMPACT OF BELIEF:
LEARNING TO TAKE CONTROL OF YOUR LIFE

LIN CONKLIN

AMETHYST MOON
PUBLISHING

The content of this book is intended to help those in need of hearing its message. Please remember that no self help book, friend or coach can ever take the place of a good counselor, psychologist or psychiatrist when one is needed.

The Impact of Belief: Learning to Take Control of Your Life

An AMETHYST MOON Book

Published by Amethyst Moon Publishing

P.O. Box 87885

Tucson, AZ 85754

www.amlifecoaching.org

ISBN 978-0-9792426-2-5 (13 digit)

0-9792426-2-2 (10 digit)

Cover photography by Kristina Moorhead ©2006

THIS BOOK IS OFFERED TO YOU IN MY GREAT HOPE THAT IT CAN HELP YOU FIND WHATEVER IT IS YOU ARE LOOKING FOR.......

CONTENTS

Introduction

There are two things that determine the kind of life we lead. The first is where and how we are born, i.e., the time period, family situation, physical characteristics (gender, handicaps, etc). Once we are born, the second thing that determines how our life progresses is our belief system. Simply stated, what we believe determines how we live. Until you understand and accept that fact, you will be a product of your beliefs without even realizing it. What does this mean? It means that whether you are rich or poor, healthy or ill, happy or forlorn, what you believe has caused these experiences.

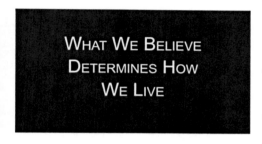

WHAT WE BELIEVE DETERMINES HOW WE LIVE

THE IMPACT OF BELIEF: *LEARNING TO TAKE CONTROL OF YOUR LIFE* explains how to shift what you believe in order to create the life you want. It contains the four-step process that has been proven to work in designing and living your life as you want it to be, which is what God and the Universe have always intended for you. You will discover how what you believe not only drives your behavior, but also draws your experiences and circumstances to you. No matter what your current situation, you will benefit from the knowledge this book contains. If you currently lead a happy, fulfilling life, then use this book to understand why that is possible and how to maintain such a life. If you are presently living a life full of pain or misfortune, use this book to discover how your beliefs are causing your life to be this way. If you want to know more about changing or enhancing your life, then use this book to learn to let go of the beliefs that hold you back in your learning and evolution. Through this book you can learn to shed old, unbeneficial habits and behaviors leading to a newer, stronger sense of self and the ability to change your circumstances.

I want you to know the purpose of your life and how to make the most of your time here on earth. It is also my wish for you to discard self-destructive actions and habits in order to replace them with healthy, productive behaviors so that you can reap the joy available and waiting for you. Our lives are full of choices which are set before

> **Our Lives are Full of Choices so that We can Evolve, Learn & Become Closer to God**

us so that we can evolve and learn in order to become closer to God. When you accept this fact and decide you do not want to be a victim of chance, then you can take control of your life in a way that gives you more confidence, helps you to attain your goals and leads you to discovering your life's mission.

If you follow the steps outlined within these pages, they will help you to discover and live the life you imagine you should be living. You will learn that you do not need to be a victim of your circumstances, but instead you can have great power over what you experience in your life.

Once you understand how much you ask for and cause the events of your life, you will be better able to achieve your goals, whether they are to better develop your friendships, become a better parent, improve your health, find the right career, or enhance your martial arts ability. The process is the same regardless of the area or areas of our lives we want to change, improve upon or eliminate.

> **Consciously or Unconsciously We Ask for and Cause All the Events of Our Lives**

We act out what we believe every moment of every day -- whether or not we are conscious of doing so. Increasing your awareness of how you affect your life through your beliefs, thoughts and actions gives you the chance to choose to take an active role in your life. When you understand how you play an active role in those things you experience, you can begin to better manage your life to both achieve your goals and evolve to higher levels of understanding. Once we are aware, it is up to each of us to choose whether or not

> **Taking Control of Your Life Signals God and the Universe that You are Ready Evolve**

to continue on as we always have -- living 'blind', so to speak -- or to make the choice that God and the Universe have put before you: Learning to take control of your life. Taking control of your life is your way of communicating to God and the Universe that you are making the choice to evolve.

HOW THIS BOOK IS STRUCTURED

People absorb information in a variety of ways. Recognizing this fact and realizing that books limit our experience to what we see or possibly what we hear inside our heads as we read, I have tried to offer three methods of presenting the material in this book. The body of the book is the text, which contains concepts, examples and explanations regarding what we believe, how it affects us and what we can do to take more control of our lives. The main points and concepts have been highlighted in black boxes with white text to both emphasize them and to make them more easy to find later for reference or review. Because many of the ideas presented may be new to you, examples that help to clarify them are included in boxes outlined in black. Here are examples:

> **THESE BOXES CONTAIN MAIN POINTS OR IMPORTANT CONCEPTS**

EXAMPLE: THESE BOXES CONTAIN EXAMPLES

This type of box will show up periodically. Its job is to help to provide an everyday example to clarify the point or concept being discussed. You may find you do not need further explanation and decide you don't need to read the examples contained in this type of box.

At the end of this book you will find an appendix that you can use to record your beliefs, behaviors and progress as you step through the process detailed in THE IMPACT OF BELIEF: LEARNING TO TAKE CONTROL OF YOUR LIFE.

The Formation of Our Belief System

Belief systems are initiated at birth, if not sooner, and continue to form as we mature. Belief systems can be defined as the collection of rules and facts that we accept as being true. We process all the inputs and stimuli we receive in every moment of every day through this set of rules and facts. Our own, personal belief systems act as the filters through which we make sense out of everything we hear, smell, see, taste, and touch. When we encounter something new, we form our thoughts and opinions about it based on and within the rules and facts that make up our personal belief system.

> **Belief Systems can be Defined as the Collection of Rules and Facts that We Accept as Being True**

We are born into a family that has an established belief system. Whether the family is a traditional mother and father, adoptive parents or an orphanage, the family we are exposed to has a belief system within which they operate. As babies and young children this first exposure to the rules, facts and boundaries the family believes and uses begins to help us form our own beliefs, even though we are not necessarily conscious of it happening. As children we almost unquestionably take clues from our parents that influence our belief systems.

The effects of our family's belief system continue to influence our beliefs as we grow up. We learn what behaviors are acceptable at home and in public. We are exposed to everything from etiquette (or the lack thereof) to attitude. We react to our parents' beliefs whether or not they say them out loud. We know what is acceptable to them and what is not. Since people choose friends with similar belief systems, our parents' friends will have most of the same beliefs as our parents. We will be exposed to others that share the same values and ethics that we witness in our homes, and so those beliefs will be reinforced even more.

Interaction with others gives us opportunities to review the beliefs our families have demonstrated and then decide for ourselves what our own belief will be. For example, if we are playing with another child and both want the same toy, we will learn about the

If your mother explains you must share and demonstrates sharing by taking a toy from you and giving it to another child, you see the behavior she would like you to have. She gives you a different toy and explains that you should play with it instead. It is her belief you should share. However, when she leaves the room and the other child rips your toy out of your hands and will not share, you clearly know that this child does not believe he/she needs to share. At that point you have a choice. You can decide whose behavior you will emulate. You can decide what you accept as the correct choice, and form your own belief about sharing.

rules of sharing from both our parents and the other child. In fact we may find that their ideas on sharing don't agree and get our first experience in making a choice and formulating our own belief regarding sharing (see *Example: Conflicting Influences*).

As you go through life you will find your beliefs can change based on your own experiences and choices. In the example above on sharing, you may have decided that you do not want to share and behave accordingly, but after many reprimands from your parents, you begin to believe that sharing is appropriate, change your belief (and thus change your behavior) and share.

As we mature the influence of our peers plays a large role in forming our beliefs. In fact their influence may play a larger role than our parents did. Because of our human need to "fit in", we watch our friends to see how they behave. When we see them do or say things that differ from our own behaviors, we are faced with the choice to conform or to be different. If our friends are supportive in our choice to be different from them, then our behavior is reinforced and our belief stays in tact. However, if they are unsupportive or openly opposed or even ridicule and embarrass us, then we must make the choice to ignore it, change friends or change our behavior. (See *Example: Influence of Peers*). Because our behaviors are simply an outward reflection of our beliefs, changing our behavior is a step toward changing our belief.

Serious differences between you and your peers can lead to either a stronger conviction to your beliefs or drastic changes in them. A stronger conviction means that you are choosing to hold true to your belief regardless of the reaction of your peers. Changing

---

EXAMPLE: INFLUENCE OF PEERS

If you are a straight 'A' student, believe good grades help you to get into college and hang out with friends who are also good students, then it is unlikely they will ridicule your good student status. However, if your friends are not able to get good grades, they may tease you about your A's. If the teasing is bearable, you may simply ignore them and continue to receive good grades, but if you cannot withstand their scrutiny, then you will have to make a different choice. You may decide to pick different friends or choose to not do as well in school. If you change friends, you keep your belief about needing good grades intact. If you instead decide to not do as well in school, then you have begun to challenge your belief that you need good grades.

---

your beliefs to fit in is how non-drinkers become drinkers, non-smokers become smokers, non-religious youth pick up religion, and so on. The influence of peers can be positive or negative, but either way it is a choice.

Another large factor in forming and altering our beliefs is societal norms. In other words, the beliefs of the culture in which you live greatly influence your choices and beliefs. If you live in a society that stresses the need for a high school education, then you are more likely to conform and complete high school. If society stresses a dislike for nose rings, then few people will have them.

By far, the media is one of the most influential tools in forming or changing the beliefs of a society. Because there are so many forms of communication in today's world, it is relatively easy to reach the masses and affect their beliefs. A good example is the effective use of the media to sway voters in presidential elections or to direct public opinion on things like war. Through the use of television, magazines, newspapers, radio, and the internet, millions of people can be given information – true or false – that alters the course of history. Most people want to conform and avoid confrontation or simply have not been exposed to a variety of ideas and beliefs, so the media is successful in swaying beliefs.

As you go through life all of your experiences will be interpreted through those things you believe to be true. When something cannot be explained within your existing belief

---

EXAMPLE: CHALLENGING OUR BELIEFS

Let's say our belief is that fire is hot and will burn us close to immediately if we place our arm into a burning flame. Now let's say Tom does not hold the belief that fire will burn him immediately. Tom believes his arm would have to stay in the burning flame for at least twenty seconds in order to produce a burn. We laugh at what seems to be naiveté on Tom's part, but sure enough, he puts his arm in a burning flame for fifteen seconds and pulls it out. He is not burned and our belief system is challenged. We can choose to believe he must be using some trick – perhaps some special coating he places on his arm to protect it – or we can choose to reevaluate our own belief and consider the possibility that fire does not burn the skin immediately.

---

system, then you will either discount it or, if you are open-minded enough, challenge your belief.

When we challenge our beliefs – even if we don't change them – it aids in our growth and evolution because it opens our minds up to possibilities that otherwise may not have been considered. In the example box (*Example: Challenging Our Beliefs*), we could take things a step further. For instance, it is interesting to wonder that if we truly did not believe fire was hot, would it be?

Although our belief systems can continue to form, alter and build throughout our lives, the baseline is established during our formative years. Most psychologists would agree that the personality and basic morals and ethics are ingrained in a person by about age seven. So it stands to reason that belief systems are also in place in that same time frame.

Experiences after this would have to be significant enough that the established belief system would ever be challenged.

BEING WILLING TO CHALLENGE OUR BELIEFS IS HOW WE EVOLVE

THE PROCESS TO TAKE CONTROL OF YOUR LIFE

It is exciting and encouraging to know that you can have more effect and control over your life than you may ever have realized. In order to affect a change in your circumstances or environment, you must start with yourself. The ability to improve your life, making it more meaningful and joyful, begins with a commitment to make a change. You must be willing to take an honest look at your role in who you are and where you are. You bring upon yourself your circumstances and experiences in order to learn and evolve. To change what you experience, you must discover what you believe and how it drives your behavior (actions and reactions) and your choices. You need to be willing to discard the beliefs that do not serve you -- without judgement -- and replace them with healthy, positive beliefs. When you change your beliefs your behavior will also change because behavior is a reflection of what you believe.

> BEHAVIORS ARE AN OUTWARD REFLECTION OF OUR BELIEFS

The Four Steps

You can change your beliefs or alter your behavior by following four basic steps:

> 1. Commitment to Change
>
> 2. Recognition of Belief
>
> 3. Challenging Belief
>
> 4. Changing Belief

It can be daunting to accept the tremendous power our belief system has had over our choices, our interpretations of others, our attitude, and our life's direction. Even more concerning is the possible limitations it may have wielded over our life with us naïve to its power. With the awareness of its existence and the knowledge of how significant it is, we can walk away with great hope. We can uncover beliefs we may not even have known we held simply by studying our choices, our predicaments and our behavior. We no longer need to be held under the spell of our belief system if it does not serve us. We can make the choice to be more aware of it, and challenge it when it does not serve us. We can take control of our lives and create the life we want.

ONE CHOICE CAN CHANGE A LIFE™

STEP 1: COMMITMENT TO CHANGE

In order to free ourselves from unwanted behavior and unwanted beliefs, we must first be aware they exist. Once we accept the fact that they do exist, then we can begin to take control of our lives. When we go on a quest to identify these behaviors and their underlying beliefs, we must let God and the Universe (or whatever higher power you believe in) know we want to make a change so that they can collude in our favor. This announcement is made through our honest commitment to change.

> **GOD & THE UNIVERSE WANT TO COLLUDE IN YOUR FAVOR**

The Purpose of the Commitment

Taking the time and making the effort to declare a commitment to change is important and meaningful. It accomplishes several things:

- Announces to God and the Universe that you are ready to do the work necessary to make improvements and take control of your life

- Puts you in the proper frame of mind to be more conscious of your actions, reactions, behaviors, and beliefs

- Lets your psyche know change may be coming and the change is okay and welcome

- Declares your intention in a more serious and definite way, which improves your chances of sticking with it and being successful

Announcement to God and the Universe

When you announce your intention to God and the Universe, they hear you clearly. Both want nothing more than to collaborate in your favor. This does not mean that everything you decide you want or intend to do will take place. Remember, they are in collusion with you to help you succeed. Since we do not always know what is best for us -- sad but true -- they are watching out for and trying to protect us. Sometimes it is ourselves we need protection from, so they intervene and try to direct us in a way that helps us to learn and evolve. It is our job in this collaboration to listen and pay attention so as not to miss the communication, which is far easier said than done. When we are in the throes of trying so very, very hard, we often miss the communication.

> OUR JOB IN THE COLLABORATION WITH GOD IS TO PAY ATTENTION TO THE COMMUNICATION

Many people wonder how God, the Universe or whatever higher power you recognize communicate to us. The methods of communication are as varied as the people receiving them, but there are some common techniques that are often overlooked. Some of these include butterflies in your stomach, the 'little voice in your head', a song on the radio, and a friend or stranger's words. Other methods also occur that may be specific to your training and background. Examples of these include communication through animals or symbols that appear in your dreams.

When we think God is no longer communicating with us, it is usually because we have failed to listen or the method of communicating has changed. I know I spent time in my life discouraged because the information that the Divine gave to me through vivid dreams or pictures and stories during meditations suddenly stopped. I believed I no longer was receiving any communication from God. Had I not gotten lost in my own sadness at such a nonsensical prospect, I might have looked back in my journals sooner than I did. Even though I know the Creator does not abandon us so, I still let my despair drive my thoughts until I stumbled across a dream I had recorded that clearly spelled out that the way I received communication was going to change dramatically. Although God had communicated this fact to me, I had forgotten. It was not that God and the Universe had abandoned me. It was that I was not paying attention to the new method of communication.

EXAMPLE: HOW THE UNIVERSE COMMUNICATES

Jacob has been training people in outdoor skills for the last decade. One of these skills includes tracking. Because Jacob spends so much time studying animal tracks, he also knows their habits. Jacob has been struggling with the direction of his life. He is unsure whether he is meant to continue to teach outdoor skills or if he needs to take on a more conventional job. He poses this question to God. Three days later Jacob is walking through the woods when he comes across a fox. He is quite surprised to find the fox is sitting squarely in front of him and staring at him, not running or showing any signs of concern for Jacob's presence. Jacob stops and stares back. After several minutes the fox gets up and leisurely strolls away.

Most people would be stunned and excited by their experience, but to Jacob he had received an answer to his prayer. He knows that foxes have incredibly good hearing, smell and sight. He would never have seen this fox unless it wanted to be seen. Jacob also knows that the acute senses the fox possesses are the types of senses he needs to be a good outdoor skills instructor. Jacob knew that this fox was a message and an answer to his question, which he interpreted to mean that he should continue to teach.

Nature skills are a big part of Jacob's life, so when he asked the Universe for a sign if he should continue to teach outdoor skills, it is no surprise that his answer came through an animal. For others with a different background, this form of communication would not work; it would be missed. God would not choose this method for someone who would be unable to decipher the message.

Proper Frame of Mind

In order to stick to a commitment you need to believe there is a reason to invest your time, energy and effort -- especially if you are already stretched thin. If you do not believe you will receive any benefit from this book or the process it contains, then it is very unlikely you will complete the steps. In order to be successful at making changes and taking more control of your life, you have to be prepared mentally to be more aware of your behaviors and beliefs. If you are not in the right state of mind, you are less likely to observe yourself as completely as you would if you were employing all of your effort and concentration rather than just some of it.

The steps require work on your part to observe yourself from an open-minded, non-judgemental viewpoint. If you do not approach this method from that perspective and frame of mind, you run the risk of getting bogged down in self-judgement instead of moving forward to making change.

Prepare the Psyche

We hold on tight to our belief systems because they are the controlling force behind our actions and reactions. They are the framework within which we operate and the filter through which we see the world. Good or bad, positive or negative, we are comfortable within our belief systems because they bring order to our lives. Through them we know what to expect and how to act.

The prospect of changing the system can disturb us more than we know. Our psyche must be notified that we want and need to look at our beliefs in order to evolve. Moving from the known, familiar belief system to an unknown one needs to be accepted by our psyche. When we alter a belief it can often feel uncomfortable to us because it changes our old, familiar behavior. It can take time to let a new behavior and belief become comfortable. It is a natural, protective response for the psyche to try to disallow or discourage any change. Signing the psyche up to help and not hinder reshaping beliefs is very beneficial.

Focus Intention

In a world full of distractions it is easy to lose focus. Bills need to be paid, kids need to be fed and homework needs to get done. There is always an endless sink full of dishes (at least there is at my house) and finding time to spend with your friends can be a struggle. Amongst all of your real life duties and considering all those things you want to do, finding the time to work on beliefs and behaviors can be challenging. When you consciously declare a commitment, you are agreeing to find the time to focus your attention on improving yourself. With all that needs to get done in your life it can seem like just one more burden. Instead of looking at it that way, imagine that you are going to change your belief about being too busy to the point that you create free time. Know that when you complete the steps described in this book that you can end up changing your life enough that the time you need becomes available. Investing the time to change your behavior and learning to attract those things that aid in your evolution instead of those things that drain you of your precious resources is time well spent.

The Contract

You can think of this commitment to discover and change old, unwanted behaviors and beliefs as a contract. I like the word 'contract' because it is defined to be a binding agreement, which cannot and should not be undertaken lightly. Depending on your life experiences, the way you react to the words 'commitment' and 'contract' will vary. Some of you like the idea because you know it will help you to see the process through to completion. However, I realize that others are feeling very uncomfortable with the thought of having to make a commitment or agree to a contract. If you fall in the latter category, then your reaction, which is a behavior, can be your first opportunity for learning. The behavior you have is discomfort toward the idea of commitments

> **THE STRONGER YOUR COMMITMENT TO CHANGE, THE MORE GOD & THE UNIVERSE WILL RESPOND**

or contracts. You will learn later that your behavior (actions and reactions) represent your beliefs. In this case your reaction represents a belief you have that does not favor commitments and/or contracts. Moving forward in this four step method means you will have the chance to assess your belief regarding commitment and contracts. In order to continue the process to be able to change your behavior and beliefs, could you accept and agree to go through a process whose purpose is to help you to learn to take control of your life? If you agree, then even though you haven't overtly made a contract, but still follow through and recognize, challenge and change your belief, then there may still be enough of a commitment (although silent) to succeed. Without some level of commitment, you will never complete the process to effect change.

The stronger the commitment you make, the more God and the Universe will respond. That is why I'd really like you to make a contract to announce your commitment. This contract can be made between you and God. You can also make the contract between the part of you that wants to change and the part that needs to change. What is the difference between the 'want' and 'need' parts? The part that *wants* to change is open to the idea that change is a possibility and may even be excited about what that can mean in your life. It is the part of you that is willing to go through the work that will be required to effect change.

> **IT CAN BE MORE COMFORTABLE TO KEEP UNHEALTHY BEHAVIORS & BELIEFS THAN TO FACE THE UNKNOWN RESULTS OF A NEW BELIEF**

The part that *needs* to change may be (and most likely is) secure with the belief system you already have in place. Even when our belief systems drive unhealthy behavior, we are still more comfortable with the known than the unknown that exists when we make a change. Although unhealthy behavior and belief systems are not serving us, they make us feel secure because we know what to expect. We know what actions are born out of our belief and what reactions happen because of it. More importantly, we know the reactions and judgements of others when we act out the belief. (See *Example: Security of the Known*).

Change and the unknown consequences of change can be frightening. It could mean rejection by friends and family, which we may not be ready to handle. It is often far easier to hold on to old, habitual behaviors.

It takes a huge amount of courage to face the unknown. Most people create the worst possible scenario instead of the most favorable when they do not know what is going to happen. Perhaps it is a leftover automatic response from more primitive times. It is this type of behavior -- your reaction to the fear of the unknown -- that you will discard through your commitment to change. Making the choice to commit to ridding yourself of those behaviors and beliefs that no longer serve you is a huge step in your evolution.

EXAMPLE: SECURITY OF THE KNOWN

Many people remain in abusive situations long after they have recognized the relationship for what it is. When you ask them their reason(s), they will tell you they can't leave, they have no place to go, they can't afford to leave, or it's really not that bad. These statements are the verbalizations of what they believe, and so they are absolutely true for them at the time they say them. Deep-seated beliefs are hard to see or admit.

Often there is some part of the abused person that wants to get out of their relationship, but another part holds on to the security of their current belief and that keeps them stuck repeating the cycle and not knowing how to break it. To those in the abusive situation who have not yet been able to challenge and change the belief that is keeping them there, there appears to be no solution that will release them. The part of them that is comfortable with the known (i.e., they know what abuse is like and what the results are) wins out over the part that is fearful of the unknown (i.e., what will happen if they leave). It takes a shift in belief -- which is not at all easy -- for them to be able to change their circumstances. Some catalyst is needed to help them see what other possibilities and outcomes exist in order to take enough fear of the unknown away that they can build a new belief. Challenging and changing their belief then allows them to break the relationship.

MAKING THE CHOICE TO DISCARD BELIEFS THAT DO NOT SERVE YOU IS A HUGE STEP IN YOUR EVOLUTION

STEP 2: RECOGNITION OF BELIEF

Background Beliefs

Many of the beliefs that drive our behavior operate without us being aware of them. In other words, we seldom give them much thought because they have become so unconditionally accepted we do not ever think of challenging them. I call this type of belief a 'background' belief because they remind me of the kinds of computer programs, like anti-virus software or operating software, that operate in the background while you are using a computer. You are pretty much completely unaware they are running, yet the role they play controls how well your computer will operate.

We learned about our world by being part of a family, whether that was a traditional two parent household, a single family situation or other living arrangements. We also learned from our experiences as part of a school, church, synagogue, club, or neighborhood.

Background beliefs can include simple things like knowing that the sun will come up tomorrow morning. Seldom does anyone go to bed and worry about whether or not the sun will rise in the morning. It is not a belief you think about challenging because you accept it as a fact that is very unlikely to change in your lifetime. Many background beliefs reside within your own belief system. Most of these were imprinted into your belief system when you were young. They may have been taught to you by your parents or other respected adult, inherited as part of a family or genetic system, picked up from being part of a certain culture, or learned by being exposed to a particular environment.

> BACKGROUND BELIEFS
> ARE SO DEEPLY ACCEPTED
> AS TRUTH THAT THEY
> ARE SELDOM, IF EVER,
> CHALLENGED

Taught or Accepted Beliefs

When we are very young we rely on our parents for guidance to help us form our own belief system. Their knowledge of the world and how it operates is passed to us. Many of the beliefs they impart operate in the background of our every day lives when we get older; they help us function in a relatively safe environment even though we no longer think about them. A simple example of the formation of this type of taught or accepted background belief is given in the example box (*Example: Forming an Accepted Background Belief*), which uses fire and what we accept as true about it to demonstrate a belief that is seldom challenged and pretty much held throughout our lives. It is not a belief we think about needing or wanting to change, so it operates in the background (i.e. we seldom think about it or challenge it) as a truth. When you need to make a choice about using your hand to grab your burger off the grill or use tongs, you don't have to think very long or hard about using the tongs.

Unless we are some how mistreated when we grow up, we trust our parents, teachers and most other adults. Because of this trust, when we are young we pretty much accept what they teach us as truth. They may consciously instruct us through what they tell us or show us. They also unknowingly pass on some

---

EXAMPLE: FORMING AN ACCEPTED BACKGROUND BELIEF

When you are first exposed to a fire or to a hot stove you do not yet have a belief about it. If you tried to touch the fire (or stove), someone probably intervened to stop you and told you, "No. Do not touch. It is hot." You may have accepted this at first, but if you did not accept the fact that fire or a stove could be hot and hurt you, you may have touched it anyway or you may have accidentally come into contact with fire and found out first hand that it is best not to touch it. Your experience with fire or a hot stove showed you that touching fire had its consequences, which became part of your belief system. More than likely you formulated the belief that fire is hot and can cause you harm. For most people this belief is held throughout their lives and they make the choice to keep a safe distance from a fire. As we grow up we do not need to continuously test fire to see if it is hot. It is a background belief we hold as a truth.

background beliefs. These are unconsciously demonstrated through their actions and words. We are simply witnesses to the behaviors. Being exposed to accepted behaviors and beliefs, whether overtly taught or inadvertently witnessed, imprints these same things into our belief systems as truths. They are one element of what makes up our ethical and moral standards.

Some examples of beliefs and behaviors we accept and mimic (at least in our early lives) include suitable ways to treat others, boundaries of personal space, acceptable public demonstrations of affection, appropriateness of lying, being late or on time, or how you greet another person (hug, handshake, nod, etc.). See *Example: A Belief That is Taught* in the concept explanation box.

EXAMPLE: A BELIEF THAT IS TAUGHT

Beliefs that we are taught and include in our own belief system are often taken for granted because they were such a natural part of our every day life growing up. Men who were raised to open doors for women do so without second thought, especially if their behavior was often positively recognized and reinforced. Even if later in life they are challenged for their behavior and decide to change it, they will most likely feel a little odd the first few times they don't open a door for a lady.

Beliefs that we are taught and include in our own belief system are often taken for granted because they were such a natural part of your every day life growing up. Actions and behaviors we carry out without second thought, especially if the behavior was repeatedly complimented, encouraged and reinforced, become comfortable and seem natural to us. Even if later in life these accepted beliefs are challenged and we decide to make a change, the new behavior will most likely feel a little odd the first few times we use it.

WE LEARN BETTER WHEN WE ARE TAUGHT THE SAME THING MULTIPLE WAYS

Beliefs that are taught to us at a young age can make the greatest impacts on our belief systems. It is at this time that our beliefs are forming and we are most impressionable. If the behavior we witness matches what we are told, then we receive the same information in two different ways: hearing and seeing. Learning stays with us longer when we receive it in multiple ways, so if what we see matches what is said, it is more likely to be accepted as true and learned.

When we are young and someone tells us that it is wrong to lie, we believe them at face value. If we watch this same person always be truthful, then it reinforces that standard. We both heard them say that telling the truth is appropriate and then saw them behave in concert with what they told us. However, the opposite belief can be just as heavily reinforced if we witness them lying. We were told lying is inappropriate, but the same person that told us that was seen to lie. Now our belief may not be what they are telling us, but instead what they are showing us. Remember, what we do speaks far louder than what we say.

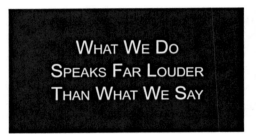

WHAT WE DO
SPEAKS FAR LOUDER
THAN WHAT WE SAY

Cultural or Environmental Beliefs

Besides being a product of our home conditions, we are also influenced by the other environments to which we are exposed. If we are sheltered and kept from the world, then our belief systems tend to be more rigid due to lack of exposure to alternative beliefs. Our view of the world has been protected and we may not be able to comprehend ideas or standards that fall outside of our belief system. On the other hand, when we have been shown a variety of lifestyles, living situations, conditions, cultures, and beliefs, we have the opportunity to be more open-minded and accepting of other ideas and ways of being. That does not mean that we will be more broad-minded; it just means we had more of a chance to be so because we were introduced to more experiences.

Some of the more prevalent local environmental exposures include schools, day care establishments, religious organizations, grandparents' homes, cities (or towns or rural settings), and cultural events (plays, concerts, etc). Each of these is filled with differences in people and, therefore, differences in beliefs. (See the example box, *Example: Environmental Influence*).

EXAMPLE: ENVIRONMENTAL INFLUENCE

Most children attend school where they are exposed to many different beliefs and behaviors. It does not take long for teenagers or even younger kids to discover they are judged by what they wear, who they associate with and how they act. The desire to fit in is strong in most humans, so the influence of the experiences that occur at school can be more powerful than the lessons received at home.

If a young girl, Sally, is made fun of for wearing shorts with flowers on them, then she is less likely to wear them again. She has learned that what you wear affects how others treat you. Sally's belief system has been influenced by her experience of being teased. As a result, she forms a belief that what you wear will determine whether or not others accept you.

This same young girl wants to be part of the popular crowd at school. From her previous experience, Sally knows that how she dresses is one element of being accepted by the popular crowd. She buys the 'right', acceptable clothes and works to be included. She is ecstatic when she is 'lucky' enough to gain the right to be included.

Unfortunately, the group of popular kids she has chosen to become part of believes you need to drink to be 'cool'. Sally has never discussed drinking with her parents because they never considered the possibility that Sally, at her age, would be faced with any choices about drinking. However, the group she is now part of drinks excessively. At first she refuses the alcohol she is offered, but that leads to being teased. Sally knows she is too young to drink and that it is illegal, but she wants to fit in. Her experience of rejection when she wore flowered shorts and the belief that resulted from that experience are now an influence in her decision about drinking in order to fit in. She elects to drink, is praised for her choice and continues to be accepted as part of the popular group for her choice, which reinforces the behavior. This experience adds to her belief that what you wear determines your acceptance, and Sally now believes that she must drink alcohol to be accepted. Sally's environment has taught her these beliefs and probably many more.

On a broader level they include the country we come from and the ethnic heritage to which we belong. Society carries with it large belief systems that we either adhere to or rebel against. When we are growing up we get clues from our parents and other influential adults in our lives as to what is acceptable, which again influences our own belief regarding conforming or rebelling to society's beliefs.

> **CONTINUAL EXPOSURE TO OTHERS' EXPERIENCES CAN INFLUENCE OUR BELIEFS AS IF WE HAD GONE THROUGH THE EXPERIENCE OURSELVES**

We learn what our country of origin believes about its friends and foes and can either adopt the same beliefs or work to alter them. Once again, the contact we have with people that are for or against our country's beliefs will impact our own belief. The same is true for those of common ethnic heritage or religious affiliation.

Just as with taught or accepted beliefs, cultural and environmental beliefs can be learned from direct experience or by exposure to others' experiences. They do not need to be explicitly told or shown to us for us to pick them up.

Inherited Beliefs

Many of our beliefs come from our experiences within our family structure, whatever that may look like. In today's world there are numerous possibilities -- step parents and step siblings, parents of the same sex, traditional two parent families, single parent situations, extended families (grandparents, aunts, uncles, cousins), etc. Other beliefs are inherited through our constant contact with other systems or groups, such as clubs, churches, neighbors, and schools.

When you are growing up you are surrounded by a variety of belief systems that agree in some areas and collide in others. You inherit many of your beliefs through your exposure day in and day out to such systems. Even if you have not had the direct experience yourself, the fact that you are in constant contact with people who did have first hand experience gives you an exposure to the experience. When your parents, teachers and community hold a belief and somehow repeatedly demonstrate or relate their experiences to you, you often take on this belief as your own. In other words, the indirect experience is enough to affect your belief system. In the example box, *Example: Inherited Belief*, you will find a belief that some people hold even though they never had any direct exposure to the experience that originally formed the belief.

EXAMPLE: INHERITED BELIEF

From about the 12th to as late as the 16th century there were numerous attempts by Europeans to recover the Holy Lands from the Muslims. These raids, attacks and wars were called The Crusades. Muslims that inhabit that region today still know and feel the devastation The Crusades caused. Even though The Crusades occurred over five hundred years ago, the environment is still one that holds on to how negative the experience was. The belief about The Crusades causes many Muslims to feel a reaction today. In fact it is strongly advised that you avoid the use of the word 'crusade' when traveling in the Middle Eastern region because of the negative feelings it generates for many Muslims.

More and more it is becoming an accepted truth that our ancestors' abilities are passed to us through our genes. If that is true then is it not also possible that their beliefs are remembered in our genetic structure? If it is true that we are evolving, then we must have the ability to remember the information and lessons we have gained during this evolution. Can you consider the possibility that the soul, which is eternal, has the responsibility to bring our previous lessons to us? If you can accept that possibility, then it is not far to go to believe that we hold information in our cells that came from our experiences in previous lifetimes or in other dimensions, including the remnants of the beliefs we held.

Although there can be a fine line between beliefs that are taught or accepted, cultural or environmental and those that are inherited, it is not important to brand the belief. What is important is to be able to recognize that your behavior is driven by values, ethics and morals that are derived from many sources. By exercising your free will you are responsible for keeping those beliefs that support you and jettisoning those that are unhealthy and do not serve you.

Hidden Beliefs

All of your experiences are interpreted through those things you believe to be true. When something cannot be explained within your existing belief system, then you will either discount it or, if you are open-minded enough, challenge your belief. Because

> THERE ARE BELIEFS WE KEEP HIDDEN FROM OURSELVES THAT DEEPLY AFFECT OUR BEHAVIOR

our beliefs play such a large role in our lives, it stands to reason that we should know what they are -- at least those with the most impact. You may be aware of some of them already. The strong beliefs we hold are usually fairly easy to identify. An example of a strong belief would be your view that murder is wrong. However, there are beliefs we keep hidden from ourselves and do not even know, on a conscious level, that we hold them. These are harder to identify, but it can be extremely important that we do so.

Uncovering Hidden Beliefs

Whether we want to accept the following fact or not, it is true: *We behave in accordance with what we believe.* (See *Example: Behaving in Accordance with Our Beliefs*). When you can accept the fact that you are driven and, in a sense, controlled by your belief systems, then you have an opportunity to change those parts of your life that you do not like. With only a few exceptions, if you do not like your current job, environment, habits, or whatever else, you have the power to re-create these areas of your life. It all starts with what you believe.

> #### EXAMPLE: BEHAVING IN ACCORDANCE WITH OUR BELIEFS
>
> If we believe we are fat, then when we look in the mirror we see someone who is overweight. If we believe we are a good parent, then we become defensive if someone makes a negative remark about our parenting style. If we believe we are an excellent skier then we shun the bunny slopes and opt for the double black diamond ski runs. If we think of ourselves as someone who does not lose, then our behavior is always to win. The examples go on and on and show up in our personal and professional lives.

In my own case I did not realize how much I was concerned -- and believed -- that I would be judged by what I was doing when a member of my family came home. I did not want them to find me 'just' reading or watching a movie because then they might think that was all I'd been doing all day. How silly is that? Not so much. I know I'm not alone in harboring concerns about what others might think.

If this belief had not been so strong and so hidden from me, then I would have thought about their reaction, dismissed it as not needing to impact my plans, and done whatever I had planned to do. Had this been the case, I would have affected a change in my belief system that said I need not concern myself with their judgement. However, in my case the belief was stronger than I realized. In fact it was so powerful it adversely affected my behavior. I would not read, watch a movie, sit quietly to meditate, or engage in any other activity I judged to be 'non-productive' because some member of my family might 'catch' me not working. There was always something that needed doing, so I pushed myself constantly and got lost in the 'doings' of my life -- working, cleaning, outdoor work, etc. A lot got done...and I got more and more exhausted. My belief that I would be judged in a negative

> WE BEHAVE IN ACCORDANCE WITH WHAT WE BELIEVE

manner if someone discovered I was not working was causing nonsensical behavior. However, until I recognized it, I had no ability to change it. Once I was able to identify the behavior, I then had the opportunity to identify and examine the belief that was causing it. That belief was hidden from me and borne out of a series of experiences that occurred when I was very young and impressionable. The belief that I was not good enough never found its way to my consciousness until I went searching for it. The circumstances that gave birth to this belief are unique to me -- the important piece is knowing that this particular negative belief is shared by many of you reading this, even though our backgrounds and life experiences are not common. A belief like this one is hard to admit, but once you can face it and see that there need be no judgement against yourself for having such a belief, then you can challenge its validity.

In my case I realized that my family was not judging me to be lazy or non-productive. I was placing that judgement on myself due to the belief I held. In fact when I could finally see that I realized that my family already knew I had a tendency to work too much, so they probably would have been overjoyed to find me doing something to relax. And even if they didn't, why should that bother me? I knew I didn't just sit around all day doing nothing! These realizations allowed me to challenge and change the inaccurate, hidden belief that caused the behavior I no longer wanted to engage in.

To stop my undesirable behavior meant I had to first be aware of it. Once I recognized the behavior, then I could be more conscious of the thought process I went through which led to uncovering the underlying belief. At that point I could challenge the belief and decide if I was willing to change it.

Using Behavior to Recognize Belief

Knowing that our behaviors are a reflection of our beliefs means we can use our behavior to uncover those beliefs we do not even realize we have. Often they operate so automatically that we do not even think about them as beliefs. The example I gave about how concerned I was that someone might catch me not working was not something I took time to think about even though it had been affecting my behavior for years. It was only when I opened up and asked God and the Universe to help me uncover beliefs that were adversely affecting my life did I create the environment in which I was willing, able and open enough to discover them. So, the first step to discovering your hidden beliefs is the true, real desire to do so. Once you have made the commitment to recognizing the behaviors and beliefs you would be best served by changing, then you can start looking at your behaviors with a different eye and ear.

> WE CAN DISCOVER OUR HIDDEN BELIEFS BY MONITORING OUR BEHAVIOR

Discovering our hidden belief systems requires a conscious effort to watch and monitor our own behavior. The way we behave is how we act out our beliefs. So, it stands to reason that by learning to observe and analyze our behavior, we can uncover even those beliefs we do not know we hold.

There are various methods you can use to observe your own behavior depending on your personal preferences, likes, abilities, and most effective way of learning. Whatever method you decide on, it needs to be one that you will both remember and want to do. Just like an exercise routine or New Year's resolution, if you do not pick a process to discover your hidden beliefs that you can tolerate enough to stick with, then your chances of completing or continuing it are slim.

> EVERY BELIEF IS A PRODUCT OF YOUR UNIQUE EXPERIENCE

It is very beneficial to learn to observe yourself with enough detachment that you can recognize and record your behaviors without feeling the need to label them as 'good' or 'bad'. There is no benefit to using your time or energy dwelling on the feelings of guilt, self-doubt, sadness, or anger that may surface. Use these feelings to decide whether or not your behavior should be modified, but do not get lost in them. In other words, we must be very cautious not to get trapped in <u>over</u> analyzing or punishing ourselves for our past conduct. This process is intended to help you know your belief system, not to judge it. Remember every belief you hold is a product of some experience you have had. Everyone has had positive and negative experiences that have resulted in some beliefs they like and some they dislike. Because you have the power to change the belief, you do not need to waste your resources (time, energy) in placing judgements on your beliefs or the resulting behavior they have caused. Instead save your time and energy to make a positive change to what you believe and your outward behavior will follow accordingly.

> DON'T WASTE YOUR VALUABLE RESOURCES -- TIME & ENERGY -- JUDGING YOUR BELIEFS

One way to observe yourself and your habits is to rely on your dominant sense. If your dominant sense is seeing, then your best observation mode would be to watch yourself and your behaviors. What I mean by this is to look out through your eyes as if they are not your own, but instead belong to someone else. What are you doing and are you comfortable with your actions?

If your dominant sense is hearing, then you would listen to yourself speak and observe yourself as if you were someone else listening to you. It is not the individual words you focus on; it is the message the words are conveying. How do you react to what you are hearing? Is it pleasing or bothersome to you?

If you need to experience or feel, then monitor how your body reacts to what you say and do. What are the sensations that occur? Do you feel at ease, secure, unworried, or happy or do you feel tension, anxiety or irritated?

By observing yourself in a detached manner, you have a better chance of freeing yourself enough to make observations without making judgements. Your job is to observe and note your behavior, not deem it as 'good' or 'bad'. You simply want to recognize what behaviors you would like to alter so that you can examine the beliefs that are causing them.

Another option to uncover a hidden belief is to identify the actions that take place when you find yourself in a situation you do not like or that somehow makes you uncomfortable. How did you get there? What choices did you make (i.e., what behaviors, actions and reactions did you engage in) that led to being there?

RECORDING YOUR BELIEFS HELPS YOU TO MONITOR YOUR PROGRESS & EVOLUTION

Whatever method you use to recognize behaviors you'd like to understand or change, be sure to record them. You can use a journal, a notebook, a voice recorder, or a even scrap piece of paper (don't lose it). It does not matter how you keep a record. What is important is that you keep one. As you work through changes in beliefs and behavior, you will find you are training your mind and body to be more aware of your actions and ethics. This means you will recognize more behaviors and beliefs than when you were unconscious of their existence. Unless you have an incredibly good memory, finding a way to record your findings for review later can be quite helpful. It aids in reminding yourself of how far you've come and how much you've evolved.

It is not necessary to record every single behavior you observe. That would prove impossible since you are doing, thinking, seeing, feeling, hearing, etc., every moment.

You only want to record those behaviors that invoke a sensation of looking wrong, sounding inappropriate or feeling undesirable. These are the behaviors that you will focus on in order to challenge the hidden belief(s) that cause them. Those actions, habits and behaviors that are acceptable to you can be left alone for now.

Because this exercise could become overwhelming quickly, especially if you have more than one behavior you want to change, I suggest you move on to the next step when you have one to three behaviors on your list. Once you've worked through the process with those items, then you can repeat the procedure to identify the next conduct you would like to change. However, moving to the next step does not mean you stop observing yourself or your actions and reactions. Continue to record what you observe and use the list to identify the next change you'd like to make.

QUESTIONING
OUR BELIEFS IS
IMPERATIVE TO OUR
EVOLUTION

STEP 3: CHALLENGING BELIEF

Challenging a belief means that you are questioning whether or not it should continue to remain among your system of beliefs. If you accept that you are here to evolve then you need to do more than go through life without questioning the reasons for and lessons contained within the experiences you have. By going through the first two steps, *Commitment* and *Recognition*, you made yourself more conscious and aware of your behaviors and beliefs. While you were recording them, you probably decided on the behaviors and beliefs you wish to alter or eliminate. You are now ready for the next step in the process to take control of your life, *Challenging the Belief(s)*. You can begin to consciously challenge the beliefs you want to change and challenge the beliefs that lie behind the behaviors you want to transform.

How Do I Challenge a Belief?

Challenging a belief boils down to only a few questions:

1. Why do I have this belief (i.e., how does it serve me)?

2. How did this belief form in the first place?

3. What will happen if I give up this belief?

4. Do I want to change, discard or keep this belief?

How Does This Belief Serve Me?

We hold on to our beliefs for many reasons. However, generally speaking, beliefs are kept because they somehow help us in our survival. This is as true of the beliefs that are *not* healthy for us as it is of the beliefs that we need to eat and to drink water. Until we understand that we need to monitor our beliefs to know whether or not they serve us, we continue to behave and act

> BELIEFS ARE KEPT BECAUSE THEY SOMEHOW HELP US IN OUR SURVIVAL

out our beliefs even when they are unhealthy.

A belief that serves us is one that aids us in our evolution. We often think a belief is serving us until we take a deeper look. In my case my belief that work comes before pleasure appeared to be serving me. When I was part of the corporate world, I worked

> A BELIEF THAT SERVES US IS ONE THAT AIDS US IN OUR EVOLUTION

long hours and did whatever it took to complete projects on time and have them done in a way that exceeded the expectations of my bosses. For my hard work I received promotions, bonuses and accolades. Being the sole breadwinner because I was a single parent, the money allowed me to take care of my daughter and give her those things I didn't have when I grew up. The benefits of health insurance provided us with security and kept us healthy. We enjoyed fun vacations, good clothes and excellent food. I was able to treat my family and friends and put money away for when I retired.

From all appearances my belief that work comes before pleasure was serving me and others quite well, but the reality was it was both harming my health and keeping me from spending my valuable time with my family and friends. It also left no room for me to take care of myself.

When I made the decision to leave the security of my corporate job, I had begun to understand how my belief was driving me toward greater risk of health issues and how it left me feeling remorse at having missed out on time I could have spent with my daughter before she was grown or with other family and friends. By challenging my belief that work comes before pleasure, I consciously chose to invest my time more wisely, and in many ways I succeeded in doing so. It felt good and I stopped checking in on this belief.

> IT IS HARD TO GIVE UP A BELIEF THAT HAS HELPED US SURVIVE

However, until I began to *really* explore my own belief system, I did not recognize that this belief was still holding on and affecting my life today. As with many beliefs that have helped us to survive, it is hard to give them up. Sometimes we are afraid of the results and other times we are simply oblivious to the fact that we are holding on. In my case I did not recognize that I had transferred the belief from my corporate world to my own business. Once I figured that out, I put my life more in balance only to have the belief surface again. This time I didn't recognize it because it wasn't the traditional 'work' I put first, but instead it was the caretaking of my mother during the onset of dementia, my stepmother during her battle with Parkinson's, my father during his cancer, and on and on. It was not that I should not have been a caretaker. It was the way I approached it. There was always work to do and someone who needed me. Because my residual belief of work comes first still drove me, I took care of everyone and everything before I ever considered that I also needed to be taken care of.

A belief that worked well for my survival -- I could handle any project or any crisis -- was the same belief that did not serve me. The belief helped me to *survive* a difficult time in my life and focus on what needed to be done because somewhere deep down I was afraid I might get lost in the emotion of these events. I kept the belief because

> A BELIEF THAT WORKS FOR OUR SURVIVAL MAY BE THE SAME BELIEF THAT DOES NOT SERVE US

it made me feel safe, even though I did not make that choice consciously. However, the belief did not *serve* me because I failed to check on my own needs. My evolution stalled until I could take the time to feel how these events affected me and to examine what I could learn from them. Had I not recognized that my behavior was still showing me that the belief still existed, I would have continued the behavior.

What you can learn from my experience is that when you think you have changed or discarded a belief, you still need to check yourself to be sure it has not cropped up some other place in your life. Remember, beliefs that have helped us survive are hard to give up, even when we are committed to doing so.

When you challenge your own beliefs, you will need to look at them as nonjudgmentally as possible. If judgement starts to get in the way, it is harder (and maybe impossible) to really look at how the belief may be helping you to survive or feel safe, but not serve you.

Beliefs that serve you are those that allow you to stay healthy, happy and to evolve. Those that you feel you need in order to defend yourself or keep yourself from being vulnerable should be challenged. You may find they are valid and keep them or you may find they are hiding a deeper belief that needs to be understood. It often helps to discuss those beliefs you wish to challenge with a trusted friend or a life coach. If you go beyond the bounds of what a friend or coach can help you with, please consider a counselor, psychiatrist or psychologist. Looking at your belief system is your chance for some important personal growth. You can heal old wounds that you've been carrying for your entire life. You can find a way to take care of yourself, which only makes you more available and better able to serve others.

> EXPLORING OUR BELIEFS OFFERS US A TREMENDOUS CHANCE FOR PERSONAL GROWTH

Where Did This Belief Come From?

At the beginning of this book you explored the many different types of beliefs. You learned that some beliefs are taught or accepted, others are born out of cultural or environmental exposure and some are inherited. You also discovered that your belief system can be added to or changed as a result of what you experience throughout your life.

Now that you are challenging your behaviors and beliefs, it can be beneficial to look at how the belief got formed in the first place. It is *not* beneficial to get stuck in an endless quest trying to discover the belief's source. There are some cases where you may never understand where or how a belief got started. When that happens, even though it is frustrating, move forward in challenging the belief and try to let go of the desire to know its source. This does not mean you should not be diligent in your search.

> BEING DILIGENT IN OUR SEARCH FOR THE SOURCE OF OUR BELIEFS ASSURES THAT WE DO NOT MISS SOMETHING IMPORTANT

In fact you will often be required to put extra effort into locating the source, especially when it involves a hidden belief. When we think we've recognized the belief behind a behavior, yet we still have trouble changing the behavior, it is a sign that there is a deeper belief that we have not yet uncovered.

For those beliefs where you are able to discern their roots, you can use this information to uncover the many ways the belief affected your life. You can also use the discovery to help you let go of the belief if it is not serving you. In my practice as a life coach I have been fascinated by the number of people who carry a deeply hidden belief that they are not good enough. Although there are times when parents or influential adults say and do things quite consciously to lead to this belief, most of the time

> MANY PEOPLE CARRY THE BELIEF THAT THEY ARE NOT GOOD ENOUGH

it is born out of a fairly innocent act by a trusted, admired adult. The example box contains one such type of innocent chain of events that led to a belief and a lifetime of behavior unnecessarily (see *Example: The Source of a Belief*).

> ASK GOD & THE UNIVERSE TO HELP IN DISCLOSING THE SOURCE OF YOUR BELIEF...& KNOW THAT THEY WILL

A great way to find the source of a belief is to ask God and the Universe to provide you with that information. Once you've made the request remember to pay attention so that you do not miss the answer. A response is always given, however you must believe that is true in order to be able to recognize it.

In my own life, I had a particular compulsive habit that I had been working very hard to eliminate from my life. I asked for the source of this habit because I was having difficulty identifying the core belief and I felt knowing the source would help me identify the true belief behind the behavior. A few days later I found myself sitting in a coffee shop in my home town, which is a good twenty five hundred miles from where I live now. I was surprised when a teacher I had in high school came in the shop and recognized me. We had a very pleasant talk, which I thoroughly enjoyed. This chance meeting got me to thinking about the classes I'd had with him...and then it struck me. I had forgotten something he had said to me that caused me extreme embarrassment in

EXAMPLE: THE SOURCE OF A BELIEF

Amy held a belief that she was not good enough. Before she was aware of this belief, she did not recognize it as the source of her behaviors. These included being a workaholic and a perfectionist. Once Amy knew that her behaviors were an outward reflection of her beliefs, she began to look at how she acted. When she discovered how important it was to her that she do everything perfectly and that the need to do so was affecting her ability to complete her assignments at work, she decided she needed to uncover the belief that was driving her perfectionist behavior.

Amy struggled to understand what belief could cause her behavior, but with the help of a good friend she learned that she did not believe she was ever good enough. Amy spent time thinking about her life experiences and asked God to help her uncover the source of this belief. Time passed, and she received an unexpected answer to her prayer. She was spending the week visiting her parents when her father asked Amy if she remembered playing with blocks as a child. Amy thought about it and then she remembered, "Yes, Dad. I'd play for hours at a time trying to build houses out of the blocks."

She was shocked when her father jokingly replied, "I will never forget this one time I teased you about how the red blocks and the green blocks did not match. I was surprised at how you tore everything down and started over. I was fascinated at how serious you were. Then your brother came home and he teased you about how the blocks weren't the same size and you tore it down and built it again. You can only imagine how shocked I was when your sister walked in and told you that you didn't use enough green blocks! Sure enough. You knocked that house down and started again. When you went to bed I told everyone how silly it was that each of us teased you and how much effort you put into that house. We joked about it for weeks afterward."

This simple, innocent event sparked a belief that Amy was not good enough and spawned years of damaging behavior. Had Amy been present when her father explained what had happened, Amy's experience would have been different and she may never have formed the belief that she was not good enough. Her family never intended to create such a belief. It is an example of how one tiny event can affect us for years without us even knowing it.

front of my classmates. This comment was about something I was having difficulty with at home. He had no way of knowing that, and his comment seemed innocent and practical to him. He would not have ever intentionally caused me any distress. What he said was not the entire source of the belief that drove my habit, but it was enough of a reinforcement to the belief my home life was driving, that it caused me to adopt an undesirable behavior that lasted for over twenty years. I had received an answer to my prayer that could have easily been missed if I had not been diligently checking for a response.

What Will Happen If I Give Up This Belief?

> ALTERING BELIEFS EVOKES ONE OF THREE RESPONSES: NEUTRALITY, EXCITEMENT OR FEAR

Knowing that you are going to alter or eliminate a belief evokes one of three responses. You may be neutral and do not care if the belief is changed or not, you are excited about the change and are imagining the good things that will happen if you choose to give up the belief, or you are panicked at the possibility of change.

If you fall into the first category (neutrality), then you have only but to make a choice as to whether or not you will change the belief. If you are in the second category (excitement), then you are ready to move to the last step and change the belief. If you are in the last category (fear), then more work is involved.

Fear That Surrounds Some Change in Belief

Because our beliefs have helped us to survive, it can be frightening to look at the prospect of giving one up. As illogical as it may sound, this also applies to those beliefs that cause us to be self-destructive or to behave in manner we do not like.

> BECAUSE OUR BELIEFS HELP US TO SURVIVE, THE PROSPECT OF GIVING ONE UP CAN BE FRIGHTENING

One way to overcome the fear is to play into it a little bit. In other words, ask yourself what is the worst thing that could happen if you changed the belief? Let your mind wander through all of the worst possible scenarios. When you think you've settled on the worst one, then ask yourself, honestly, what if this worst scenario actually came true? These "what ifs" -- 'what if I have no place to live', 'what if I lose my job', 'what if I am rejected by my family', etc -- can keep us paralyzed for our entire lives. They can be overwhelmingly real.

> **WE UNCONSCIOUSLY WORK TO JUSTIFY OUR BELIEFS**

I ask you to consider for a moment everything you have learned about belief up to this point. You know that if you believe something, then it drives your behavior. Whatever you believe has the ability to manifest in your life. Because your belief system is the collection of things you believe to be true, those parts of you that are operating in an unconscious manner are always trying to justify these things you believe to be true. As hard as it is to admit, your own belief system can actually be working against you without you ever realizing it...until now.

Your belief system draws to you those things, experiences and people which fit into that system. If you believe that something horrible will happen, then the chances of it occurring are greatly increased. In fact by believing it you are actually helping it to happen. Now that you know that you can consciously combat that fact, which means that you can choose to not believe any of the negative possibilities. Instead you can work -- and, depending on how bleak the scenarios you've imagined, it does take work and commitment -- to redirect that energy in to imagining the best possible outcomes. Any time a thought crosses your mind about the negative things that could happen, stop the thought and replace it with a more positive and pleasant one.

> **WE ATTRACT EXPERIENCES & PEOPLE TO OURSELVES THAT FIT INTO OUR BELIEF SYSTEM**

The first few times you do this it can be a challenge, but try to stick it out. It takes time -- sometimes a lot of time -- to make a change in how we behave. Old habits can be deeply embedded and very hard to change, even when we know it is best for us to do so.

With all that said, it is still possible that your worst scenario may play out. However, it will only do so if you hold the belief that it will. If you still harbor even the smallest doubt, this doubt gives energy and belief to the fear, which can be enough to cause it to manifest. God and the Universe listen very well and give to you all that you ask for -- although not always in the way you expect it.

Do I Want to Change, Discard or Keep This Belief?

Here's where your free will gets involved. Free will is your right to make a choice without anyone else interfering. Free will is God's permission for you to make choices. Free will is about structuring our individual belief systems by choosing what will be part of that system and what will be omitted.

> FREE WILL IS GOD'S PERMISSION FOR YOU TO MAKE CHOICES

Now that you have identified the belief you want to alter or delete, you must decide whether or not you are willing to go on to the next step and make a change.

> EXERCISING FREE WILL IS HOW YOU STRUCTURE YOUR BELIEF SYSTEM BY CHOOSING WHAT IS & IS NOT PART OF IT

STEP 4: CHANGING BELIEF

This step may prove to be the hardest one because it requires an action to be taken **and** continual follow up for days, if not weeks or years. It takes conscious hard work to monitor your behavior and your thoughts. It also takes work to make corrections when old behavior, habits and beliefs creep in. It is during this time of decision when we are given an opportunity to make a choice to change or to continue with our old beliefs and behavior. Here is when our commitment to change is put to the test.

The Change Process

When you read my book THE POWER OF CHOICE: CREATING THE LIFE YOU WANT, you learn how to attain your life's purpose through a five-step process:

- Identify

- Imagine

- Intend

- Believe

- Achieve

These five steps can also be used as the tool to make changes in your belief system. The change process helps you to take the belief you have identified as needing to be changed and imagine what your life will be like with the new belief. When you intend it to be so and believe it as true, then you achieve the result of successfully changing your belief system to serve you better.

Identify

Having made it to this step (Changing Belief) means you have already been successful in identifying the behaviors and beliefs you want to change or eliminate. Now you must identify how you will modify your belief or what new belief you will adopt that will best serve you. It is a creative activity which can be approached head on -- in other words, you can work on the belief directly -- or you can approach it from the end result by deciding on the new behavior you would like to exhibit. If you choose the latter method, then once you've settled on the actions and reactions you are comfortable with, you will have to then identify what kind of belief would drive those behaviors. Confused? Check the example box *Example: Identifying Behavior to Change Belief* and refer to the section, *Using Behavior to Recognize Belief*, which starts on page 34.

Imagine

The next piece is to imagine how you will act and react if you adopted a change in your belief. When you imagine you begin to train your mind to accept the new belief as real. The brain has a hard time distinguishing from those things that are real and those things that are imagined when you truly believe what you are imagining can be and will be real. Use your imagination to place yourself in situations where your new belief and the behaviors it drives are necessary. Imagine the scenario to play out positively. If any negative thoughts, feelings or images come to mind, stop and change the scene

> IMAGINING HELPS TO TRAIN YOUR MIND TO MORE READILY ACCEPT YOUR NEW BELIEF

to a more positive one. Remember it is your fear of letting the old, comfortable beliefs go that is causing any negative reactions you are having. Do not get discouraged. Just stay focussed on imagining your new, positive, healthy experience.

Intend

According to the dictionary, when you intend something to happen it means that you are making some plans toward it. In order to make changes in your beliefs and behaviors, you must be willing to invest the effort required to make the changes real. In other words, to just make plans toward your goal of changing a habit, behavior and/or belief is not enough. In this process 'intend' is not to be taken lightly. You must focus your intention strongly in order to help manifest change.

EXAMPLE: IDENTIFYING BEHAVIOR TO CHANGE BELIEF

Mary does not like the size of her hips. Although she has a wardrobe full of dresses she has chosen to disguise what she sees as a flaw in her body, she is seldom satisfied with her appearance. In fact, Mary has a habit of cursing at the mirror every time she is displeased with what she sees reflected there.

Carmen is Mary's teenage daughter. Although Carmen and Mary have never discussed Mary's self-image, for years Carmen has witnessed Mary's behavior when she is displeased with her appearance.

Today Carmen is getting ready for her first date. Mary is helping her get ready when Carmen looks herself over in the mirror and begins to curse. "I can't go out like this! Look at how big my hips look in this outfit. He'll never want to be seen with me." As Carmen sobs and laments, Mary tries to sooth her, but her attempts to calm Carmen do not work. Mary is amazed at how much Carmen sounds and acts exactly like her when she is getting dressed.

Until this incident, Mary had never seen her own behavior. It was such a natural part of how she got dressed that she never realized how she sounded, what she said or the effect it had in teaching Carmen. Being able to see Carmen's actions was a wake up call for Mary. She knew she no longer wanted to exhibit this behavior or have her daughter go through the pain of disliking herself. Mary recognized a behavior she no longer wanted and began to work to change it.

To start Mary stayed conscious of what she said and did when she dressed, whether or not anyone was watching. If she found herself wanting to degrade herself because her appearance wasn't everything she hoped to achieve, she instead forced herself to find some other aspect of her appearance that was positive. This simple step helped her to stop the negative self-talk. With these new behaviors in place, Mary identified the belief that drove her behavior. By changing the belief that her hips must be a certain size, she can maintain the new behavior and demonstrate a more healthy self image for her daughter.

You discover how important it is to hold what you want as a real possibility and begin to remove your doubt about the reality of it happening. To intend requires commitment to truly wanting your beliefs to change. God, the Universe and all other higher powers know our hearts, so they know if we harbor any doubts. Unless you are intending

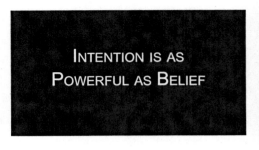

INTENTION IS AS POWERFUL AS BELIEF

something that is not yours to intend (i.e., affecting another's free will or involving a violation of universal law), then whenever something you think you are intending does not become true, it is an indication that you have some piece of doubt that you have not yet conquered.

The imagining you did in the last step helps you to solidify your intention to make a change. Intention is as powerful as belief. Those things we set our intentions on achieving can and do become reality. Intention is a way of communicating to God and the Universe that you acknowledge your destiny and are willing to progress to fulfill your life's mission.

Believe

Believing can be difficult. You may even find that the belief you are working on has other, deeper beliefs behind it. It takes work and perseverance, but looking deeper to find what really drives the behaviors you wish to discard is worth the effort and time. I understand the difficulty of believing. Even though I have seen the successes my clients have achieved when they have used this method, I still struggle with some doubts in regards to changes in my own beliefs. It is as if I cannot convince myself that it is 'okay' to 'allow' certain changes in my life. It is frustrating to know that until I decide it is alright to let go, then those areas of my life where I cling to beliefs I should discard will continue to plague me. It is my contract that keeps me committed to succeeding in changing those beliefs. It is the knowledge that I am human and imperfect that allows me to forgive myself for needing more time.

You may believe you have discovered the core belief that drives some of your behaviors, but when you alter that belief your behavior does not change completely or maybe not even at all. This is a sign that you are going to have to dig deeper. When behavior does not change after you have altered a belief, it means that you have not identified the true, core belief.

As your intentions become more solid and you decide it is okay to believe them, you will then begin to see changes in your life. As the new belief sets in, you will enjoy the benefits of its affect on your behavior and attitude. Holding your belief as being absolutely true can be difficult, but if you will allow yourself the gift of enjoying your new actions and reactions, you will know the effort of maintaining your commitment to your contract to change was worth it.

> **WHEN BEHAVIOR DOESN'T CHANGE AFTER ALTERING A BELIEF, THE TRUE, CORE BELIEF WAS NOT IDENTIFIED**

Achieve and Celebrate!!

Don't forget to give yourself credit for your achievements, no matter how small or big. Celebrating even a small success in changing behavior helps to reinforce the new belief.

Celebrations don't have to be flamboyant or extravagant, unless you want them to be. Celebrations of your achievements must fit your personal style or they become stressful events -- exactly the opposite of their purpose! Celebrations may be as simple as treating yourself to ice cream or a walk. They can also be far more involved. You decide what feels best for you.

Once you have made a change, begin the process again. At first you may want to stick with the beliefs that are simpler to change, which helps to build your confidence in the process and your ability to create change in your life. Regardless of the severity of the habit or behavior, the process works as long as you are willing to look deep enough to identify the true, underlying, driving belief behind your behaviors and habits.

When Old Behavior Threatens to Return

Many of us make it to this final step (*Changing Belief*) only to fall into our old, comfortable patterns of behavior. It sometimes is just easier to do or say the same old thing rather than putting out the extra effort to recognize the old pattern, stop, correct ourselves, and then move on with a new behavior born from a new belief.

Making your way past the voice in your head that wants your attention and wants you to respond the same old way is tough and can be scary. You are making your way into unknown territory when you change your belief and behavior, which can cause fear to surface. With your old belief in place, you knew how people reacted when you behaved the old way, but you do not know what they will do or think when your new behavior emerges. Will you lose friends, be ridiculed, shunned, or ignored? Maybe. However you could be congratulated, hugged, admired, or forgiven.

When we make dramatic changes or even small adjustments in our beliefs, our outward actions and reactions also change. These changes and adjustments often cause reactions in our family and friends. As we alter our belief system, then we are seen by others as changing. Reactions from our family and friends can range from compliments to anger, jealousy to abandonment. When we discard negative or self destructive attitudes and behaviors, we sometimes find that our current group of friends cannot accept our decision to change. We may even lose some of these relationships when we stay committed to our contract to change.

> PRAYERS ARE ALWAYS ANSWERED -- JUST NOT ALWAYS THE WAY WE EXPECT

In many cases we find that our friends are not truly our friends at all or that we have changed enough that our interests are no longer in common. When a drug addict decides to stop taking drugs, he or she may find that their drug-addicted friends do not accept their decision to stop taking drugs, especially if the relationship is based on the taking of drugs. For the person that has made a choice to give up their addiction, it takes work to break free and believe that new friends with common interests will emerge. They will, given time and a commitment to the belief that they will.

It can be extremely hard not to abandon your new beliefs and run back to your old habits. If you are finding it difficult to stick with your commitment, find a support system to help you. Ask for help from family and friends. If they cannot or will not accept your decision to make changes, then seek out support from individuals going through similar adjustments, a good counselor or a member of the clergy. If you ask God and/or the Universe for support, then it will be provided. Just remember our prayers are always answered, just not always the way we expect. You need to keep your senses attuned so you do not miss the help or support you have requested when it shows up.

Awareness Leads to Growth

The 4 Steps
1. Commitment to Change
2. Recognition of Belief
3. Challenging Belief
4. Changing Belief

Once you have been through this process or even while you were using it, you may notice that there are many factors that cause you to challenge your beliefs all the time, but before you became conscious of the impact of belief you were unaware that it was happening. With the four steps at your disposal, you can design and form your life as you like. Just keep in mind that you do not have the right to affect another person's free will or to harm another. Also remember that what you ask for is given, just not in the form or in the way you may have expected. I remember a dear friend of mine who wanted to learn how to handle difficult employees. By saying this out loud to me, she in essence asked the Universe to help her learn the ability to deal with unruly people. Over the next few months some of the most negative, difficult, disruptive people were transferred into her group and placed under her supervision. My friend was forced to learn how to deal with some of the most difficult employees she ever came across. Of course when she asked to know how to handle this type of subordinate, she never meant she wanted the experience firsthand -- but what better way to learn!

YOUR THOUGHTS, PRAYERS & WORDS HELP TO CAUSE THE LIFE LESSONS YOU EXPERIENCE

Remaining aware of our thoughts, prayers and requests helps us to manage what lessons are placed before us. Our growth and evolution is enhanced by our experience.

Awareness of What We Draw to Ourselves

Even though we attract those people, things and happenings to ourselves that we need for our evolution, we can miss some lessons and chances for growth. This is because we interpret everything through the filter of our belief system, which has been formed and altered by our previous experiences. A lesson may be right before our eyes, but we remain unable to see it because our interpretation of the event can only be processed through those rules and truths we hold. This fact is not meant to discourage you, but instead inspire you to seek out and challenge your belief system regularly because when our belief system changes, then we often see the same experience a whole new way. This new viewpoint leads to growth and evolution.

> **OUR BELIEF SYSTEMS CONTROL HOW WE INTERPRET OUR WORLD & EXPERIENCES**

Using our new beliefs, it is a good idea to think through those experiences that have remained most influential to us. These are the ones we often tell to others or are those that we frequently think about. If you ask God and the Universe to bring those life incidents to mind in order for you to look at interpreting them from a new perspective, then your request will be honored. Again, pay attention once you've made such an appeal so as not to miss the response.

Impact of Past Lives

Depending on your beliefs about evolution and the eternalness of the soul, you may want to consider using the lessons you brought with you into this life from your previous lives. There are many books available to help you look more deeply into the effects of your experiences and relationships that may be holdovers from other lifetimes.

Continuing Impact of Experience

By now you understand that our belief systems are constantly being either reinforced or placed into question by our experience. This is true because it is the belief system that drives every action we take or reaction we have. As we have discussed throughout this book, experiences come in many forms and can influence us whether through our direct or indirect involvement.

> OUR BELIEF SYSTEM
> IS CONSTANTLY EITHER
> REINFORCED OR DISPUTED
> BY OUR EXPERIENCE

IN PARTING...

Beliefs drive your actions and reactions. They are behind all of your motives, they filter all of your experiences and can be the only thing that keeps you from attaining your dreams. What you believe controls your ability to be the best you can be at whatever it is you are working to be the best at (martial arts, painting, singing, parenting, driving.... it does not matter).

Changing your beliefs can make a huge impact in your life. You can turn around a life that seems bleak and make it into a beautiful experience instead. The only caution I issue is to understand that some things put into motion over years and years may change course, but may not be able to be completely mended. I suppose it will hinge on your level of commitment and belief and the laws of the universe. Can you reverse a serious illness or a loss of a limb? Maybe with enough belief you can or maybe you chose to go through such difficulties because you thought it would aid you in your evolution and learning. Those questions are yet to be definitively answered, but whether or not you can completely heal such wounds, changing your beliefs surrounding them will certainly have an effect on your life, your experience of those circumstances and your effect on those you encounter.

Once we are born, our life is driven by what we believe. Using the information presented in this book, you can shift what you believe in order to create the life you want, with God and the Universe at your side. Let go of the beliefs that are not allowing you to learn and evolve. Discard the old, unbeneficial habits and behaviors and give way to a newer, stronger sense of self. Know that you own the ability to change your circumstances. Know that you can discover the purpose of your life and make the most of your time here on earth. Knowing that you are not a victim of chance, you can take control of your life in a way that gives you more confidence, helps you to attain your goals and leads you to discovering your life's mission.

Now that you are aware that you have been given a choice by God and the Universe, do you choose to reveal THE IMPACT OF BELIEF in your life?

ONE CHOICE CAN CHANGE A LIFE™

APPENDIX

> **The 4 Steps**
> 1. Commitment to Change
> 2. Recognition of Belief
> 3. Challenging Belief
> 4. Changing Belief

I encourage you to record your progress through the four steps. I have found that looking back at my own progress months and even years later gives me even more insights than I recognized at the time, which furthers growth and evolution.

Step 1: Commitment to Change

The Stronger Your Commitment to Change, the More God & the Universe Will Respond

Writing down your commitment to change forces you to put more than a few seconds thought into it. The written commitment can be used daily as a kind of mantra, which will solidify the contract you made to change. By periodically reciting it you help your mind to accept it and continue to let God and the Universe know you are serious in your endeavor to transform yourself in a positive way. It also provides you something concrete to refer back to it when you need a little boost to continue the process.

Examples of Commitments to Change:

"I commit to identifying and changing those beliefs that no longer serve me."

"I am thankful for identifying and altering or discarding my unhealthy beliefs."

"I am grateful for the positive, healthy changes in my belief system."

Please notice that there is no use of words like 'will', 'going to' or 'want to'. The meanings of these words all have a negative connotation. In other words, they are phrases that still leave open a possibility that you may not change. They put the action(s) you will take into the future instead of the present. When you are 'going to' do something, it means you have not yet begun to do it. When you pray or speak using these or similar words, you are not demonstrating a firm commitment. Instead use positive, present tense words. In the examples these words are 'commit', 'thankful' and 'grateful'. These connote the belief that these things are already beginning to happen or have happened.

My Commitment to Change -----

_____

_____

_____

STEP 2: RECOGNITION OF BELIEF

EVERY BELIEF IS A PRODUCT OF YOUR UNIQUE EXPERIENCE, and

RECORDING YOUR BELIEFS HELPS YOU TO MONITOR YOUR PROGRESS & EVOLUTION

To keep this process manageable, continually record the behaviors or beliefs you recognize as those you wish to change, but you move on to the next step (*Challenging Belief*) when you have one to three behaviors and/or beliefs on your list. Once you've worked through the process with those items, then you can repeat the steps to identify the next belief or behavior you will address. Space is provided to record both beliefs and behaviors.

The beliefs I'd like to change or eliminate -----

_____

_____

_____

_____

_____

_____

_____

_____

_____

WE CAN DISCOVER OUR HIDDEN BELIEFS BY MONITORING OUR BEHAVIOR

The behaviors I'd like to alter or eliminate -----

_____

_____

_____

_____

_____

_____

_____

_____

Take time to prioritize your lists, selecting the first belief you would like to challenge. If you have a behavior you would like to challenge, but you do not know the underlying belief, you can use the Challenge process questions listed on the next page to help identify the belief. You can also refer to the section, *Using Behavior to Recognize Belief*, which starts on page 34.

STEP 3: CHALLENGING BELIEF

QUESTIONING OUR BELIEFS IS IMPERATIVE TO OUR EVOLUTION

Challenging a belief means that you are questioning whether or not it should continue to remain part of your belief system. If you feel it is driving non-productive or negative behavior, then it is time make a change.

Once you have identified the belief you want to challenge, ask yourself four questions and record your responses in the spaces provided.

Four Questions

1. Why do I have this belief (i.e., how does it serve me)?
2. How did this belief form in the first place?
3. What will happen if I give up this belief?
4. Do I want to change, discard or keep this belief?

Why do I have this belief (i.e., how does it serve me)?

BELIEFS ARE KEPT BECAUSE THEY SOMEHOW HELP US IN OUR SURVIVAL

You may have kept a belief because it made you feel safe or secure even though it did not help you to grow or evolve. Answering the question of how a belief served you can be difficult. Take time to contemplate the reason(s) you needed this belief.

This belief helped me by -----

_____

_____

_____

_____

How did this belief form in the first place?

BEING DILIGENT IN OUR SEARCH FOR THE SOURCE OF OUR BELIEFS ASSURES THAT WE DO NOT MISS SOMETHING IMPORTANT

Use this question to look at the experiences and circumstances of your life. When you think you have identified how this belief formed, try to look a little deeper or a bit further back in your history to be sure you do not miss the true, root source of this belief. Record both when and how it was formed.

This belief formed when -----

_____

_____

_____

_____

_____

_____

_____

_____

_____

What will happen if I give up this belief?

ALTERING BELIEFS EVOKES ONE OF THREE RESPONSES: NEUTRALITY, EXCITEMENT OR FEAR

Keep in mind that it is natural to want to justify the need for our beliefs. Be mindful of the response the idea of challenging this belief elicits. Your reaction will be a clue as to how difficult challenging the belief will be. A neutral or excited response usually indicates that you should have little difficulty, whereas fear indicates that changing the belief my require more effort. To prepare for the change ahead, list what you think could happen (both positive and negative) when you alter the belief.

If I give up this belief ----

Do I want to change, discard or keep this belief?

FREE WILL IS GOD'S PERMISSION FOR YOU TO MAKE CHOICES

Having looked at why you hold this belief (how it served you), how and why it was created and what will happen if you give up this belief, you now get to exercise your free will and make the choice to change the belief, eliminate it from your belief system or continue to hold it as true.

I choose to < *change   discard   keep* > this belief.

STEP 4: CHANGING BELIEF

If you chose to keep or discard the belief, then you are ready to select the next belief or behavior and repeat the steps. If you chose to change the belief, then continue the process of change.

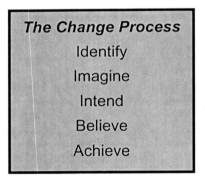

The Change Process

Identify

Imagine

Intend

Believe

Achieve

Identify

EXERCISING FREE WILL IS HOW YOU STRUCTURE YOUR BELIEF SYSTEM BY CHOOSING WHAT IS & IS NOT PART OF IT

You made it to this point because you identified the belief you are about to change. Now you get to formulate your new belief. Be innovative, imaginative, open-minded, and have fun with this creative process. Do not get stuck by trying to get it perfect. If the new belief needs to be altered because it does not result in the new behavior you want, you can modify it and improve upon the new belief at any time. By imagining the new belief in the next stage (Imagine), you will have plenty of opportunity to refine it.

My new belief is -----

_____

_____

_____

_____

Imagine

IMAGINING HELPS TO TRAIN YOUR MIND TO MORE READILY ACCEPT YOUR NEW BELIEF

Try out your new belief by imagining what new behaviors (actions and reactions) it drives. Imagine yourself in scenarios where the new belief will be used. Record both the situations where the belief will come into play and your new behavior in those circumstances.

I imagine my new behaviors to be -----

_____

_____

_____

_____

_____

Intend

Intention is as Powerful as Belief

Intention involves how you feel, what you think about and how you behave. It requires you to be conscious of any negativity or doubts that might arise so that you can change them into positive thoughts, feeling and behaviors. This does mean you ignore them, but instead help yourself to understand the power a negative thought or a doubt can have. They can destroy the chance you have to make a change.

For example, if I believe I can walk across a log suspended across a river but then begin to have doubts, I create the possibility of falling. I might think, "I will not fall," but this still allows for 'falling' to be a possibility. I can alleviate this doubt by replacing it with seeing myself successfully negotiating the log or by thinking, "I can walk across this log successfully." Both are acts of intention. You may wish to use this space to document how you alter any doubts that may arise.

I intend -----

_____

_____

_____

_____

_____

_____

_____

Believe

WHAT WE BELIEVE DETERMINES HOW WE LIVE

Record any changes or refinements to your new belief here and refer back to it if you falter and need a reminder. Staying true to your new belief takes time and effort. Remember your contract for a Commitment to Change.

My new belief is ----

_____

_____

_____

_____

Achieve

WE BEHAVE IN ACCORDANCE WITH WHAT WE BELIEVE

Don't forget to celebrate your successes!!!

I celebrated by ----

_____

_____

_____

_____

_____

NOTES

NOTES

Breinigsville, PA USA
21 February 2010
232850BV00001B/2/A